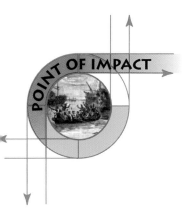

POINT OF IMPACT

The Boston Tea Party

Rebellion in the Colonies

KAREN PRICE HOSSELL

Heinemann Library
Chicago, Illinois

Designed by Roslyn Broder
Printed in the United States by Lake Book Manufacturing, Inc.

07 06 05 04 03
10 9 8 7 6 5 4 3 2 1

Library of Congress Cataloging-in-Publication Data
Price Hossell, Karen, 1957-
   The Boston Tea Party : rebellion in the colonies / by Karen Price Hossell.
        p. cm. -- (Point of impact)
Summary: Recounts the events leading up to the colonists' defiant act against the British known as the Boston Tea Party and describes the event itself, showing how it ultimately climaxed in the American Revolution.
Includes bibliographical references and index.
   ISBN 1-58810-906-2 (HC), 1-40340-534-4 (Pbk)
   1. Boston Tea Party, 1773--Juvenile literature. [1. Boston Tea Party, 1773. 2. Massachusetts--History--Colonial period, ca. 1600-1775. 3. United States--History--Colonial period, ca. 1600-1775.] I. Title. II. Series.
   E215.7 .P75 2002
   973.3'11--dc21
                                      2001008695

Acknowledgments
The author and publishers are grateful to the following for permission to reproduce copyright material:
pp. 4, 11, 16, 26, 28, 29 Bettmann/Corbis; pp. 5, 6, 7, 10, 13, 14, 15, 17, 18, 20, 21, 23, 25 North Wind Picture Archives; pp. 8, 19, 22, 24, 27 The Granger Collection, New York.

Cover photograph (T-B) by Bettmann/Corbis.

Every effort has been made to contact copyright holders of any material reproduced in this book. Any omissions will be rectified in subsequent printings if notice is given to the publisher.

The author would like to thank her parents, her husband, David, and her editor, Angela McHaney Brown.

Some words are shown in bold, **like this.** You can find out what they mean by looking in the glossary.

Contents

The Boston Tea Party

In the early evening of December 16, 1773, about 50 Boston **patriots** dressed as American Indians walked down Milk Street in Boston, Massachusetts. Their faces were blackened with burnt cork, and they had blankets wrapped around their shoulders. A crowd of supporters and people who were simply curious followed the men.

This is one of many illustrations of the history-making event that took place in Boston Harbor.

Many people of Boston looked out of their windows to see what was going to happen. They knew one thing: It was all about tea. The crowd grew larger as the group marched toward the wharf.

The raid begins

Three ships were tied up at the wharf: the *Dartmouth, Eleanor,* and *Beaver.* The crowd watched silently as the protesters broke into three groups. Each group went aboard a ship. Some ran down to the hold—the storage area below the ship's deck—to find the tea chests. Some waited above, hatchets in hand. The men in the hold attached the chests to rope. Other men pulled the chests up to the deck, where still others broke the chests open with hatchets. Once the chests were broken up, they scooped out the tea and threw it into the water.

This illustration shows the colonists dressed as American Indians during the Boston Tea Party. It took less than three hours for the men to destroy the tea chests and toss all the tea into the water.

By nine o'clock they had broken open 342 chests and thrown 90,000 pounds (48,024 kilograms) of tea into Boston Harbor. In a few short hours the Boston Tea Party was over. Its effects, though, would be felt not only in the thirteen colonies but also 3,000 miles (4,828 kilometers) away in England.

The next morning, some of the men had to dump tea out of their boots before putting them on. In the harbor, small boats were sent out to break up the thick coating of tea leaves that floated on the water.

Taxing the Colonies

Many of the earliest colonies in North America were settled by a group of people who had left England so they could worship more freely. By 1700, there were thirteen colonies in North America. Boston, a city in the Massachusetts Bay colony, became an important port city, where ships could sail in to unload and reload goods. Like the other twelve colonies, Massachusetts had its own form of government. The people elected representatives and sent them to Boston, the colony's capital, where they voted on laws. But the colonies still had to answer to England's lawmaking body, called **Parliament.**

Acts of Parliament

England had lost a lot of money from 1754 to 1763 fighting the **French and Indian War.** To help pay for the war, Parliament began to pass acts, or laws, to tax the colonists. The first was the Sugar Act, passed in 1764. It required colonists to pay three pennies for each gallon of molasses, a sweetener shipped into the colonies. In 1765, Parliament passed an act that forced colonists to help support British soldiers who were in the colonies to keep peace. Because it included payment for the soldiers' quarters, or rooms, it was called the Quartering Act.

This is a British tax stamp used in the North American colonies.

Most colonists agreed that Parliament had the right to make laws relating to the goods that were traded between England and the colonies. The passage of all the acts together, though, made them worry. Some colonists thought that if they obeyed the laws and paid these taxes, they would soon become like slaves to Great Britain—forced to obey whatever laws the British government decided to pass.

The Stamp Act

Parliament passed another act in 1765—the Stamp Act. The act forced colonists to pay to have a stamp put on newspapers and other paper items when they bought them. Special British collectors were put in place to make sure the Stamp Act was followed. When colonists found out about the Stamp Act, many reacted violently by rioting and bullying collectors until they resigned. The reason the colonists were angry was that they were considered to be British citizens because of living in British colonies, but they were not represented in Parliament. They had no voice in the laws being made. The protests of the colonial **patriots** came down to one statement: No taxation without representation.

The Stamp Act Congress

In October 1765, nine colonies sent **delegates** to a meeting called the Stamp Act Congress in New York City. The delegates wrote a statement protesting the Stamp Act. The colonies also agreed to **boycott** British products. This meant that they would not **import** any products from England or buy British goods already in the colonies as long as they were forced to obey the Stamp Act. In response to the protests, Parliament **repealed,** or ended, the Stamp Act in 1766. Then it immediately passed the Declaratory Act, which stated that Parliament had the power to make laws for the colonies, with no exceptions.

Boston was one of the cities in which riots broke out when the Stamp Act of 1765 angered colonists.

The Townshend Act

Many in British government were not happy that **Parliament** had **repealed** the Stamp Act. They thought the repeal made Parliament look weak, as though it were giving in to the North American colonies. One man who felt this way was Charles Townshend, whose job was to oversee England's public money. In March 1767, Townshend announced to Parliament another bill that, if passed, would place more taxes on the colonists. **Duties,** taxes that were paid by **merchants** when the goods they bought were delivered to them, would be placed on glass, paper, lead, paints, and tea. With support from other members of British government, the bill was passed. The money raised from the duties would go to pay for the salaries of governors and judges in the colonies.

The British East India Company was one of the major tea distributors during colonial times.

Boycott

Colonists reacted to this new tax by again threatening to stop **importing** goods from England. Merchants in Boston started the new **boycott.** Then it spread to Philadelphia and New York. When ships from England carrying goods arrived in the colonies, they were often sent back to England. A law that was passed by Great Britain in 1724, however, stated that traders could not return tea to England once it had reached the colonies. Some merchants took merchandise and stored it in colonial warehouses instead of sending the ships back to England.

Colonists did not like the idea of giving up tea. They had gotten used to drinking it every day. For years, though, merchants had been buying tea **smuggled** in by Dutch ships. The tea smuggled in from the Dutch was cheaper, and merchants did not have to pay duties on it. Merchants continued to smuggle tea from the

Dutch even after the boycott started, so many people continued to drink tea. Usually, though, they did it secretly. The **patriots** had declared that anyone who drank tea was an enemy to his country.

Colonists continued to protest that Parliament had no right to tax them, since they had no representation in Parliament. Some members of Parliament agreed with them and tried to get the Townshend Act repealed. Finally, in 1770, Parliament agreed to repeal the act. They kept the three-penny-a-pound tax on tea, though. The colonists were pleased to have the other duties removed. They felt, however, that Parliament had kept the tea tax as a way to tell colonists that Parliament had every right to control them with taxes and other harsh laws.

The boycott continued, but merchants began to weaken. They were losing money and began to argue for ending the boycott. The Townshend Act was almost completely repealed, but many still felt Parliament should repeal the tea duty as well. As the year passed, colonists began to openly drink tea again, and merchants continued to pay the three-penny tax on each pound of tea.

A PATRIOT'S WARNING

John Dickinson from Delaware saw the Townshend Act as a sign of more dangerous things to come from Great Britain. He wrote:

"Those who are taxed without their own consent, expressed by themselves or their representatives, are slaves. We are taxed without our own consent, expressed by ourselves or our representatives. We are therefore—SLAVES."

Merchants from Boston, Philadelphia, and New York argued about whether to continue the boycott on tea.

The Boston Massacre

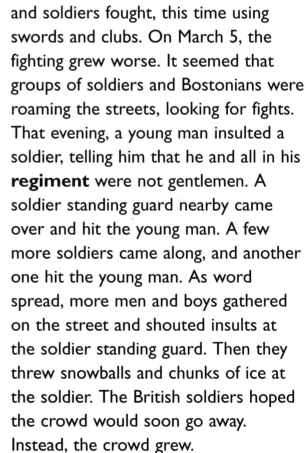

As the colonies' **boycott** against the Townshend Act was coming to a close, things were heating up in Boston. Officers who were assigned to collect the Townshend **duties** were constantly bothered by colonists. Some men looked for opportunities to start fights with the British soldiers. The soldiers were allowed to work at other jobs during their time off, and they worked for less than the average rate of pay. This angered many people in the city, who felt that the soldiers were stealing work from them.

British troops entered Boston in 1768 to **enforce** taxation laws. Some colonists were openly unfriendly to the soldiers assigned to stay in the city.

The fight begins

On March 2, 1770, a group of soldiers and Boston citizens fought after a rope maker had insulted a soldier looking for work. The next day, more citizens and soldiers fought, this time using swords and clubs. On March 5, the fighting grew worse. It seemed that groups of soldiers and Bostonians were roaming the streets, looking for fights. That evening, a young man insulted a soldier, telling him that he and all in his **regiment** were not gentlemen. A soldier standing guard nearby came over and hit the young man. A few more soldiers came along, and another one hit the young man. As word spread, more men and boys gathered on the street and shouted insults at the soldier standing guard. Then they threw snowballs and chunks of ice at the soldier. The British soldiers hoped the crowd would soon go away. Instead, the crowd grew.

Some colonists tried to stop the fighting, while others, carrying clubs and swords, came to add to it. Someone yelled, "Fire!," and men rushed into the street carrying bags and buckets of water. Finally, a British captain sent about seven soldiers to rescue the soldier being bothered. The crowd let the soldiers through, then tightly surrounded them so they could not escape. The captain ordered the soldiers to face the crowd and load their guns, called muskets. For about fifteen minutes, the crowd shouted at the soldiers to fire. One soldier was hit with a chunk of ice that knocked him down. As he stood back up, he fired his musket. For a second all was quiet. Then the other soldiers fired their muskets, hitting eleven men in the crowd. Three died right away, one died a few hours later, and another died a few days later.

The Boston Massacre was not a true massacre, but it was called one by angry colonists. The event brought out the strong feelings of hatred and anger between the British and the colonists.

A huge crowd of about a thousand people rushed through the streets of Boston after the shots were fired. The soldiers were arrested, but by that time the people of Boston were demanding the removal of all the troops from their city. The next day, Governor Thomas Hutchinson ordered the troops to leave town. People in other colonies were horrified when they heard about the Boston **Massacre.** Most agreed that the British had too much power in the colonies, and this was proof of what could happen.

The Tea Act of 1773

For a few years, things were relatively quiet in the colonies. **Merchants** bought tea and paid the three-penny **duty,** or **smuggled** tea and paid no duty at all. Colonists bought tea from merchants and drank pots of it with bread and butter and cakes. But at the beginning of 1773, Governor Hutchinson made a speech that opened old wounds.

Not represented

The governor, who was also a judge, made the speech during a General Court session in Boston. He had heard that colonists were forming **committees of correspondence** to share news and ideas about what they saw as British interference in their government. Hutchinson said the committees were not necessary. He said that colonists did not have the same rights as people who lived in England. They did not have the right to be represented in **Parliament** because they lived too far away. The people of Massachusetts reacted by calling for Governor Hutchinson's removal.

Saving the East India Tea Company

Meanwhile, Parliament was trying to find a way to save the British East India Tea Company. The company had a great deal of debt, or money it owed, that it could not pay. Part of the debt was the result of the tea **boycott** in the colonies. Leaders of the company met

The colonies were separated from Great Britain by the Atlantic Ocean and had no voice in government.

GREAT BRITAIN

NORTH AMERICA

About 3,000 miles (4,828 kilometers)

EUROPE

COLONIES

Atlantic Ocean

with government leaders to try to find a way out of the debt. The company also had tons of leftover tea in the warehouses—about 18 million pounds (8 million kilograms). To make money, the company needed to sell this extra tea. At first the company considered selling their tea to European countries. Then they thought they had a better idea. They would sell the tea to the colonies.

Parliament passes the Tea Act

Some of the leaders thought the colonies would better accept the tea if the three-penny duty were removed. But others said it would be best to keep it. After all, colonists were buying tea with the duty already. Maybe if they changed the way the duty was paid, though, the merchants would accept the deal. They could bill the merchants in England instead of sending the bills to the colonies. If the bills did not appear in the colonies, some thought, the colonists might think there was no duty at all. On May 10, 1773, the Tea Act was passed by Parliament.

Samuel Adams set up the committees of correspondence that helped join the people of Massachusetts together. They were an important tool in the American fight for independence.

The tea was to be shipped to Boston, New York, Philadelphia, and Charleston, South Carolina. The East India Company selected only a few merchants, called **consignees,** from each city to sell its tea. About 2,000 chests filled with about 600,000 pounds (272,160 kilograms) of tea were ready to be shipped to the colonies by September 1773.

COMMITTEES OF CORRESPONDENCE

In 1772, Boston **patriot** Samuel Adams suggested that the city of Boston start a committee of correspondence. The committee would write letters about issues that troubled them to the legislatures of other colonies and to leaders of cities in Massachusetts, who had set up their own committees, as well. They were especially concerned with communicating their fears that their rights were being taken away by the British government. Later, all of the thirteen colonies set up committees of correspondence. They used them to write letters back and forth to find out what steps other colonies were taking in their fight for freedom.

The Colonists Protest

As word of the Tea Act spread through the colonies, some colonists became convinced that this was the way the British government would force them to go along with the Townshend Act once and for all. Few were tricked by Britain's attempt to hide the tea **duty** by billing the **consignees** in Britain. Many colonists felt that if they allowed the tea to come into the colonies, that would send a message to England that taxation without representation was acceptable to them. They also felt that many more taxes would follow upon their acceptance of the tea.

In Philadelphia and New York, people reacted to the news of the tea shipments by printing handbills and giving them out. Then they printed large posters called broadsides and hung them around their cities. About 700 people met in Philadelphia on October 16, 1773. They adopted **resolutions** stating that the Tea Act was **Parliament's** way of forcing them to accept the duties imposed by the Townshend Act. They also declared that any colonist who **enforced** the duties was an "Enemy to his Country."

One of the main meeting places of the rebellious colonists was the Old South Church in Boston.

The people of Boston react

The people of Boston did not take action against the tea shipments until November 3, when they tried to force the consignees to resign from their jobs. Instead, the consignees met at a store one of them owned on King Street. When this became known, a crowd of people stormed into the store. Fearing for their lives, the consignees and their families fled to Castle William, a fort held by British soldiers in Boston Harbor.

The tea arrives

On November 28, the first tea-filled ship arrived in Boston Harbor. On November 29, more than 5,000 people from Boston and surrounding towns attended a meeting. In the meeting, everyone agreed that the duty must not be paid. Francis Rotch, the owner of the *Dartmouth,* got permission to unload some of the goods from his ship, but not tea. Rotch was in a difficult position. He did not want to send the ship back to England with the tea, because no tea could be sold back to England. He would have to pay for all of the tea on the ship.

For days, Samuel Adams and his **committee of correspondence** pressured Rotch into sending back the tea. On December 16, Rotch tried to get a pass from Governor Hutchinson to sail past Castle William safely, but the governor refused because he wanted the tea unloaded first. By that time, two more ships, the *Beaver* and the *Eleanor*, had sailed into the harbor with cargoes of East India tea.

War cries

Thousands of people had met at Old South Church and were waiting to hear the outcome of Rotch's meeting with the governor. When Rotch walked in and told them the ship would not be leaving Boston, Samuel Adams stood up. "This meeting can do nothing more to save the country," he said. As he said those words, the crowd heard war whoops outside. The Boston Tea Party had begun.

Rotch knew that the British soldiers in Castle William would fire at his ship with their cannons and destroy it unless he had an official pass from Governor Hutchinson.

Freedom Fighters

There is no record of exactly who took part in the Boston Tea Party. However, historians do know the leaders of the protests against taxation without representation. They know many of the names of those who took part in protests in Boston and throughout the colonies.

Paul Revere worked as a silversmith before helping to organize the Boston Tea Party. He is shown here holding a piece of his work.

Samuel Adams

Samuel Adams was a key player in the fight for freedom. Adams spoke out against the Stamp Act in 1765 and acted as spokesman for Boston after the 1770 **massacre.**

In 1772, Adams established Boston's **committee of correspondence,** and he wrote many letters to Boston newspapers about how unfairly Great Britain was behaving toward its North American colonies. Most historians agree that Adams did not actually destroy tea on December 16, but they agree that he certainly did have a part in organizing the event.

Paul Revere

Paul Revere is best known for his famous ride to warn the people of Massachusetts that the British were on their way. He made other rides as a special messenger for the freedom fighters in Boston. Revere was one of the guards placed aboard the three ships before the Boston Tea Party, and evidence shows that he did take part in the Boston Tea Party.

John Hancock

John Hancock is known as the first person to sign the Declaration of Independence. Hancock was a respected citizen, which is one reason Samuel Adams chose him to lead some of the meetings that led up to the Boston Tea Party. Hancock also led the committee that demanded that tea **consignees** give up their jobs as tea **merchants.**

John Hancock was an important leader in the American colonies. Some patriots did not trust him, though, because he seemed to change his political views.

THE LOYAL NINE

A group of some of the most rebellious **patriots** called themselves the Loyal Nine. They kept their society secret, meeting in a small room above a business in downtown Boston. The group looked to Samuel Adams for leadership, and he considered them his most important support team. The members were Thomas Chase, whose family owned the building where the group met; Henry Bass, Samuel Adams's cousin; John Avery Jr., who owned a liquor business; Stephen Cleverly, who made things out of brass; Thomas Crafts, a painter; Benjamin Edes, a printer; John Smith, another brass craftsman; George Trott, a jeweler; and Henry Welles—it is not known what he did for a living.

In 1765, the group forced Andrew Oliver, the stamp master appointed to **enforce** the Stamp Act, to resign his post. They were also responsible for some acts of violence, including an attack on Governor Hutchinson's home in 1765, and for harassing tea consignees in 1773. The Loyal Nine later became part of another patriot group called the Sons of Liberty.

Patriots and Loyalists

Those who were involved in **importing** the tea to the colonies as a result of the Tea Act were considered by **patriots** to be enemies to the country. The tea importers were surprised by the way the Boston patriots treated them. Most of the tea importers thought of themselves simply as businessmen trying to make money. Others spoke loudly against the patriot cause.

Governor Thomas Hutchinson

Governor Hutchinson was a Boston native who was seen as an enemy because of his pro-British, or **loyalist,** views. A speech he made to Boston's General Court in January 1773 made him many enemies. In the speech, he said that the colonies did not enjoy all of the rights of Englishmen, because they were so far removed from England. They could not, he said, pass laws that went against the laws of **Parliament.**

Many Bostonians believed that Governor Thomas Hutchinson was behind the Stamp Act of 1765. In response, they attacked his home and destroyed the things inside.

Frances Rotch

Frances Rotch was the owner of the *Dartmouth,* the first ship that sailed with tea into Boston Harbor. When he agreed to ship the tea, he probably did not realize how much trouble it would cause. After the *Dartmouth* arrived in Boston, Rotch became caught between the demands of the patriots, the **customs** agents, and Governor Hutchinson.

The merchants

The **merchants** who had been chosen to sell the tea in the colonies were also considered enemies, especially after they refused to resign as **consignees.** They were Thomas Hutchinson Jr. and his brother

Elisha, sons of the governor; Richard Clarke and his sons; Benjamin Faneuil Jr.; and Joshua Winslow. While they entered the business to make a profit from the sale of the tea, they were declared enemies when they refused to resign. They angered the townspeople and soon were forced to flee either to homes outside Boston or to Castle William.

Faneuil Hall in Boston was another important meeting place for those planning the Boston Tea Party.

NO SAFETY FOR CONSIGNEES

After the Boston Tea Party, the consignees were afraid to walk the streets of Boston. Ann Hulton, whose brother was a British customs agent, wrote to her friend in England:

There is no prospect of their ever returning and residing in Boston with Safety. This place and all the towns about entered into a written agreement not to afford [give] them any Shelter or protection, so that they are not only banished from their families and homes, but their retreat is cut off, and their interest greatly injured by ruining their Trade.

The Raid

The night of December 16, 1773, was one the people of Boston would never forget. For weeks they had been meeting at Old South Church and Faneuil Hall to decide what to do about the tea. Their attempts to return it to England did not work. Samuel Adams, his **committee of correspondence,** and the **patriot** group called the Sons of Liberty led the protest using every argument and possible **negotiation.** Now it was too late. On December 17, the twenty-day time limit for **duties** to be paid would be up, and **customs** agents would seize the tea. The patriots decided to take matters into their own hands.

The raid begins

Samuel Adams announced that the raid on the ships had begun. In the back of the meeting room, someone shouted "Boston Harbor, a teapot tonight!" Everyone rushed for the doors. Outside, men dressed as American Indians had already gathered.

The colonists were determined that no tea would be received in Boston. When three ships docked in the harbor, their tea was dumped overboard.

The shouting was so loud that John Andrews, a man who happened to be drinking a cup of tea at the time, went outside. He later wrote that the leader of the meeting declared it over, and many people began shouting. Then he heard three cheers, and the crowd left the meeting, making a lot of noise as it went out into the street. Then Andrews saw the "Indians." He described them as wearing blankets over their heads and shoulders. Their skin, he said, was "copper colored," and each carried a hatchet, ax, or pair of pistols.

The Boston *Gazette* reported on December 20, 1773, how quickly the patriots worked to get rid of all the tea on the ships. It also pointed out that they did so without causing any damage to the three ships or any other property.

This Boston Tea Party memorial plaque is posted on the site of Griffin's Wharf in Boston.

AT GRIFFIN'S WHARF

The crowd made its way to Griffin's Wharf, where all three ships were anchored. A sailor on the *Dartmouth*, Alexander Hodgdon, wrote this in the ship's journal:

Between six and seven o'clock this evening came down to the wharf a body of about one thousand people. Among them were a number dressed and whooping like Indians. They came on board the ship, and after warning myself and the Custom-House officer to get out of the way, they unlaid the hatches and went down the hold, where was eighty whole and thirty-four half chests of Tea, which they hoisted [lifted] upon deck, and cut the chests to pieces, and hove [threw] the Tea all overboard, where it was damaged and lost.

HERE FORMERLY STOOD
GRIFFINS WHARF,
AT WHICH LAY MOORED ON DEC. 16, 1773, THREE BRITISH SHIPS WITH CARGOES OF TEA.
TO DEFEAT KING GEORGE'S TRIVIAL BUT TYRANNICAL TAX OF THREE PENCE A POUND,
ABOUT NINETY CITIZENS OF BOSTON, PARTLY DISGUISED AS INDIANS, BOARDED THE SHIPS,
THREW THE CARGOES, THREE HUNDRED AND FORTY TWO CHESTS IN ALL, INTO THE SEA,
AND MADE THE WORLD RING WITH THE PATRIOTIC EXPLOIT OF THE

BOSTON TEA PARTY

"NO! NE'ER WAS MINGLED SUCH A DRAUGHT
IN PALACE, HALL, OR ARBOR,
AS FREEMEN BREWED AND TYRANTS QUAFFED
THAT NIGHT IN BOSTON HARBOR"

Striking Back

Immediately after the events of December 16, 1773, Governor Hutchinson wrote a report about what had happened and sent it on a ship sailing for England. That ship did not arrive in England until January 27, 1774. Another ship that had arrived a week before spread the news of the tea party.

Lord North, a government officer, recognized that the problems between Britain and the colonies were not about taxes as much as they were about "whether we have, or have not any authority in that country." If the colonists refused to pay taxes, what other British laws would they refuse to obey?

Punishment

Upon hearing of the Boston Tea Party, the British government prepared to punish the colonists. There was no way, they said, to justify what had happened in Boston. King George the Third of England told **Parliament** that they should send a forceful message to the colonies. The British government had just received the petition from the people of Boston to remove Governor Hutchinson from office. Now the people of Boston had taken this bold step.

The Intolerable Acts

In February, Parliament began to consider seriously what to do to strike back at the colonists. Parliament wrote laws that colonists would call the Intolerable Acts, because they could not tolerate, or put up with, them. First, Parliament announced a bill that would close the port of Boston to all ships except for local ships delivering food and fuel. The port would remain closed until King George decided it would reopen. Parliament would not allow him to reopen the port until the people involved in the Boston Tea Party had paid for all the tea. The bill was approved.

Then Parliament passed two more acts against the people of Massachusetts. One was called the Massachusetts Regulatory Act. This stated that any royal official accused of a capital crime in Massachusetts, such as murder or kidnapping, must be sent either to England or to another colony for trial. The people of Massachusetts would not be able to take the official to court.

The second act was the Impartial Administration of Justice Act. This act changed the document, called a charter, upon which Massachusetts based its government. The governor's council, previously elected by the people of Massachusetts, would now be appointed by the king or queen of England. The act stated that no town could hold a meeting without permission from the British government. Also, the new governor would be able to appoint or remove anyone from almost any government position in Massachusetts. The capital of Massachusetts was moved from Boston to Salem. A Quartering Act similar to the one passed earlier was also approved.

The port of Boston was closed by British authorities on June 15, 1774. This illustration shows several warships in the harbor to **enforce** the closing.

The Colonies Come Together

Parliament removed Governor Hutchinson from office and sent General Thomas Gage to serve in his place. Gage arrived on May 13, 1774, with orders from Parliament to **enforce** the Intolerable Acts and to stop any protests that began in the city.

The port of Boston is closed

The first of the acts to be enforced was the closing of the port of Boston. The order to close it had been reprinted in the May 10 edition of the *Gazette* newspaper. When they read it, Bostonians were horrified. Samuel Adams quickly met with the **committee of correspondence.** They agreed that they would not, under any circumstances, pay for the tea they had helped to destroy.

Before being made governor of Boston, General Gage had been in charge of all British troops assigned to the colonies.

Samuel Adams then wrote a letter to be sent to the committees of correspondence in other colonies. He wrote that the closing of the port was to show other colonies what could happen if they did not follow laws made by Parliament. He urged the colonies to unite, because the violation of the rights of the people of Boston was a violation of the rights of all the people in the colonies.

Other colonies react

The other colonies had already reacted positively to the news of the Boston Tea Party. When Paul Revere returned to Boston from New York a few days later, he announced that there was rejoicing in that city and also in Philadelphia when people received the news. Church bells rang, and people shouted and cheered at what the bold Bostonians had done. When a tea shipment arrived in Philadelphia, it was calmly turned away to sail back to England. The same thing happened in New York.

Immediately after the Boston Tea Party, Paul Revere rode from Boston to New York to deliver the news.

When the news of the port closing spread, the other colonies reacted in sympathy. Other committees of correspondence promised to send supplies to Boston. When Samuel Adams called for all the colonies to stop trade with England to protest the Intolerable Acts, though, not all colonists agreed. **Merchants,** especially, remembered the hardships they had suffered during the **boycotts** in response to the Stamp and Townshend Acts.

Nearly all of the committees agreed that they should hold a meeting to discuss the issues facing them. The meeting would be called the Continental Congress. Connecticut was the first to announce that it had **delegates,** or representatives, ready to attend. Soon every colony except Georgia, which was dealing with an American Indian uprising, said it would attend. Finally, the colonies were meeting as one.

The First Continental Congre.

On September 5, 1774, the First Continental Congress met in Philadelphia, Pennsylvania. The **delegates** did not wish to call for independence from Great Britain. Instead, they wanted to work out what power, if any, **Parliament** had over colonial trade. The delegates agreed that buying goods from Britain, Ireland, and the West Indies should stop as of December 1, 1774.

The Continental Association

The delegates also agreed not to use British goods until the taxes imposed upon them were **repealed.** To **enforce** this agreement, the delegates set up the Continental Association, which would be made up of committees from each city, town, and county. The association would see to it that the colonists stuck to their promise not to trade with Great Britain. Anyone who did not keep that promise would have his or her name published in local newspapers.

Patrick Henry spoke to the 56 delegates who attended the First Continental Congress in Philadelphia.

A declaration

A committee of delegates was formed to write a Declaration of Rights, stating the colonies' claims against taxation without representation. The committee concluded that the rights of the colonies were founded on the law of nature, the British constitution, and colonial charters. On October 26, the delegates ended the historic session. They agreed that, if necessary, they would meet again on May 10, 1775. At the Congress, they swore to continue to be loyal to the British king. They had also proved they could work together for a cause.

The State House in Philadelphia would later become known as Independence Hall because of the important meetings that took place there leading up to the American Revolutionary War.

GROWING CONCERNS

After the Congress, some delegates worried that there would soon be a war. Charles Thomson of Pennsylvania wrote to Benjamin Franklin that British policy was *"dragging friends and brothers into the horrors of civil War and involving their country in ruin."* As 1774 closed, many in Massachusetts felt they should prepare for war.

The Colonists Prepare for Wa

In October 1774, Massachusetts held a Provincial Congress and set up a Committee for the Defense and Safety of the Province to see that the colony was prepared for war. Massachusetts **patriot** and future U.S. president John Adams wrote at the time that the people of Massachusetts were preparing for war.

General Gage, governor of Massachusetts, wrote in a letter to Britain that the opposition to British soldiers had moved from Boston into the countryside where colonists were openly resisting British rule. He reported that the colonists were purchasing weapons and threatening British troops. Later, he wrote about the colonies uniting: "From Appearances no People are more determined for a Civil War, the whole Country from hence to New York armed, training and providing Military Stores." The colonists were ready for war.

John Adams could see that Massachusetts was preparing for war and said that, if necessary, "an Army of Fifteen Thousand Men from this Province alone might be brought into the Field in one Week."

The Battle of Lexington

On April 19, 1775, General Gage sent about 700 men to Concord, Massachusetts, to destroy a storehouse that held guns and other supplies. The mission was supposed to be a secret, but so many troops moving through the countryside were hard to miss. The colonists in Lexington, which was on the way to Concord, sent out **Minutemen,** soldiers who were to be ready to fight at a minute's notice, to face the British troops. About 450 more Minutemen were ready when the British entered Concord. When the fighting was over, 73 British were killed, 174 were wounded, and 26 were missing. Of the colonists, 49 were dead, 41 were wounded, and 5 were missing. The American Revolutionary War had begun.

A turning point

The Boston Tea Party served as a turning point in American history. The other colonies heard about the patriots of Boston dumping British tea into the harbor and realized that they were not alone in their concerns about being taxed by **Parliament** without representation. Once each colony realized that the others had the same fears, they began to feel a sense of unity. They realized that while one colony might not be able to fight Britain on its own, if all the colonies joined together, they might have enough strength and determination to achieve their goal. At first that goal was simply to send representatives to Parliament, but when they realized the British government would not allow that, they knew the next step must be independence. The Boston Tea Party had united the colonies, and now they needed to prepare for war.

SECOND CONTINENTAL CONGRESS

The Second Continental Congress was set to meet on May 10, 1775, only a few weeks after the battle at Lexington and Concord. The Congress immediately began to prepare for war. George Washington was named Commander in Chief of the Continental Army. On July 8, 1775, Congress announced to all colonists the need to fight against the British. Then it voted to approve $2,000,000 to finance the army. Boston **delegate** John Adams wrote of his desire to fight for freedom, saying, *"Oh that I was a Soldier!—I will be.—I am reading military Books.—Every Body must and will, and shall be a soldier."*

The first shots of the American Revolutionary War were fired at Lexington, Massachusetts. Each side says the other fired first. Eight colonists were killed and one British soldier was wounded. This battle was to be the first of many between colonial patriots and British soldiers.

Important Dates

1764	April 5	**Parliament** passes the Sugar Act
1765	March	Parliament passes the Quartering Act and the Stamp Act
	October	Stamp Act Congress meets in Philadelphia
1766		Parliament **repeals** the Stamp Act
1767	March	Parliament passes the Townshend Act
1770	March 5	Parliament repeals the Townshend Act
	March 5	Boston **Massacre**
1773	May 10	Parliament passes the Tea Act
	November 28	*Dartmouth* arrives in Boston Harbor with tea
	December 16	Boston Tea Party
1774	January 27	Governor Hutchinson's report arrives in London
	February	Parliament passes the Intolerable Acts
	May 13	General Gage arrives in Boston to replace Governor Hutchinson
	June 7	Declared a day of fasting and prayer by Virginia's lawmakers in support of the colonists of Massachusetts
	June 15	Port of Boston is closed by an act of Parliament
	September 5	First Continental Congress meets in Philadelphia
	December 1	All colonial **imports** to Great Britain, Ireland, and West Indies are stopped
1775	April 19	British and colonial soldiers fight at Concord and Lexington, Massachusetts
	May 10	Second Continental Congress meets in Philadelphia

Glossary

boycott   refusal to do business with or engage in other activities with a person, business, organization, or government, usually done to focus attention on a disagreement with that party

committee of correspondence committee set up during the Revolutionary era to promote communication between the colonies

consignee   person to whom a shipment is sent

customs   process by which goods are reported and may be taxed upon being brought into a country

delegate   person sent as a representative to a meeting or conference

duty   tax on imported goods

enforce   to force people to obey a rule

French and Indian War   fought between Great Britain and France in the northern American colonies from 1756 to 1763; some Native Americans fought with the French, while others fought with the British

import   bring goods from one country into another, usually to sell the goods

loyalist   someone who remains loyal to a particular cause; during the American Revolution, a loyalist was someone who remained loyal to Great Britain

massacre   killing a great number of people, who are usually innocent of any wrongdoing

merchant   shop owner or trader

Minutemen   in colonial America, Minutemen were soldiers who pledged to be ready to fight within a minute's notice

negotiation   process of discussion and compromise with another party to achieve a goal

Parliament   supreme lawmaking body in Great Britain

patriot   person who supports his or her country; during the American Revolution, those who fought for freedom from Great Britain

regiment   military unit

repeal   officially remove or recall a decision or law

resolution   formal statement expressing an opinion or stand on an issue made by a group

smuggle   secretly bring something into an area illegally

Further Reading

Isaacs, Sally Senzell. *America in the Time of George Washington.* Chicago: Heinemann Library, 1998.

Kroll, Steven. *The Boston Tea Party.* New York: Holiday House, 1998.

Smolinski, Diane. *The Revolutionary War Home Front.* Chicago: Heinemann Library, 2001.

Index